# Rich and Poor

## Rebalancing the Economy

by Charles M. A. Clark
and Sr Helen Alford, OP

*All booklets are published thanks to the
generous support of the members of the
Catholic Truth Society*

CATHOLIC TRUTH SOCIETY

PUBLISHERS TO THE HOLY SEE

# CATHOLIC SOCIAL TEACHING

*Series editor: Stratford Caldecott*

In the one hundred years after Pope Leo XIII the world changed more than in the several hundred years before him. The pontificate of Pope John Paul II brought new intellectual resources to bear on the questions and problems of modernity, resulting in a further consolidation and transformation of Catholic Social Thought. The tradition of social encyclicals was integrated within a wider and deeper vision of the renewal of society and our place in the natural world. The social teaching of Pope Benedict XVI has built on these foundations and continued this analysis.

In the 21st century the foundations of civilised society are under threat as never before, and there is a new hunger prompted by recent events for wise and authoritative teaching on how to live together in peace and justice. The booklets in this series aim to point readers to these teachings, and will explore elements of the social doctrine of the Church that are increasingly recognised as essential to the flourishing of the human community.

# Contents

---

## References:

*Catholic Social Thought documents:*

RN   *Rerum Novarum* (The Condition of Labour) Pope Leo XIII, 1891.

QA   *Quadragesimo Anno* (After Forty Years) Pope Pius XI, 1931.

MM   *Mater et Magistra* (Christianity & Social Progress) Pope John XXIII, 1961.

GS   *Gaudium et Spes* (Pastoral Constitution of the Church in the Modern World) Second Vatican Council, 1965.

PP   *Popularum Progressio* (On the Development of Peoples) Pope Paul VI, 1967.

LE   *Laborum Exercens* (On Human Work) Pope John Paul II, 1981.

SRS  *Sollicitudo Rei Socialis* (On Social Concern) Pope John Paul II, 1987.

CA   *Centesimus Annus* (On the Hundredth Anniversary of *Rerum Novarum*) Pope John Paul II, 1991.

CSC  *Compendium of the Social Doctrine of the Church*, Pontifical Council for Justice and Peace, 2004.

CDE  *Caritas Deus Est* (God is Love) Pope Benedict XVI, 2006.

CV   *Caritas in Veritate* (Charity in Truth) Pope Benedict XVI, 2009.

# Introduction

## A world divided

When the death of the pop star, Michael Jackson, was announced, there was a frenzy of reaction, and an estimated billion people watched his memorial celebration. On the same day an estimated 25,000 children under the age of five died from mostly poverty-related causes (9 million a year)[1], without fanfare or ceremony. The contrast between the obsessive attention paid to the lifestyles of the rich and famous and the indifference shown to the world's poor, both in life and death, is indicative of the gap between the rich and the poor, a gap that transcends economics and politics, defines education and culture, determines health and well-being and in the end establishes, in a very real way, who counts as a person for us and who does not.

Yet, surely for all people of goodwill, and for Christians especially, the growing gap between the rich and the poor is a scandal that screams out for justice. We are presented, as Pope Benedict XVI has said in his latest social encyclical, *Caritas in Veritate*, "with choices that cannot be postponed concerning nothing less than the destiny of man" (n.21). The gap between the rich and

poor is not an act of nature, like the weather, something
we can complain about, but cannot effectively change.
Our DNA does not include a rich or poor gene. Wealth
and poverty are created by human actions and structures;
they reflect the choices we make, as individuals and
collectively as citizens, and the choices made by those
who came before us, the results of which we simply
inherit. Our choices and actions influence our individual
economic success or failure, but they also affect the well-
being of countless others, many of whom we never meet,
just as others actions will affect our well-being. Yet the
biggest factor that will determine our economic status is
who our parents are, and where (in which country) and
when (in which historical period) we were born into.
None of us can claim credit for these "happenstances".

As Christians we know that everything we have flows
from God's selfless gift of creation, a gift we can never
"earn" or repay, and a gift that is given to all of God's
children. As St John Chrysostom stated: "God in the
beginning made not one man rich and another poor. Nor
did he afterwards take and show to one treasures of gold,
and deny the other the right of searching for it. Rather, he
left the earth free to all alike."[2] God did not give creation
to those with political, military, social or economic power.
Humans are "co-creators" in the process of wealth
creation, and they determined the economic, social and
political institutions that determine how wealth will be

divided up, thus creating the gap between the rich and the poor. The income gap can also be a gap between life and death, hope and hopelessness, dignity and degradation, inclusion and exclusion. The processes by which societies produce "social output" have a great influence on the character of that society, and on who can hope, who has dignity, and who counts.

| Two Different Realities | |
| --- | --- |
| Reality of Poverty | Reality of Wealth |
| The poorest 40% of the world's population accounts for 5% of global income.[3] | The richest 20% accounts for 75% of world income.[8] |
| In 2005, almost 1.4 billion people lived below the international poverty line, earning less than $1.25 per day.[4] | The world's billionaires - just 497 people - were worth $3.5 trillion (over 7% of world GDP).[9] |
| 1.02 billion people do not have enough to eat.[5] | Over one billion people are overweight.[10] |
| 1.1 billion people have inadequate access to water and 2.6 billion lack basic sanitation. 1.8 billion people consume around 20 litres of water per day.[6] | In the UK the average person uses more than 50 litres of water a day flushing toilets (total average daily usage is 150 litres, 600 litres for the average American).[11] |
| $550 billion has been paid in both principal and interest over the last three decades, on $540 billion of loans, and yet there is still a $523 billion debt burden.[7] | World military expenditure in 2007 was estimated at $1.339 trillion.[12] |

## Continuing world hunger

*"Hunger still reaps enormous numbers of victims among those who, like Lazarus, are not permitted to take their place at the rich man's table"*

Pope Benedict XVI (*Caritas in Veritate*, n.27)

The persistence of world hunger in the face of decades of rising per capita food production (creating even greater abundances at the tables of the rich), shows that the central problem is not a shortage of food production, (in fact in rich countries we often pay farmers *not* to grow food so as to keep food prices higher), but instead is caused by the methods and institutions used to determine who eats and who starves. Hunger is just one form of poverty, and just as hunger is not caused by a shortage of food, poverty in general is not the result of overall scarcity. God has fulfilled His promise of abundance. Our not following His will (human sin) is at the root of all the causes of poverty.

Degrading levels of poverty are not only to be found in poor countries, but also within the emerging and rich countries. Inequality has been rising in most countries over the last 30 years.[13] The causes of this rise in inequality, both between rich and poor countries, and between rich and poor within the rich countries, can be traced to globalisation and "neo-liberal" free market policies, as well as changes in tax policy, social welfare systems and the general reduction of protections for workers and supports for the poor, all with the intention of making the economy more internationally competitive. The restructuring of economies to make them more "credible" to financial markets is called "money manager capitalism," in which the real economy (production of goods and services) serves the interests of the financial sector.

Finance is supposed to be a means to an end, a tool that makes firms more productive, helping to promote the common good. When finance as a means becomes "the end", the link between wealth creation and well-being is broken. Thus we have seen speculators gambling on food and oil futures, creating an artificial bubble in food and oil prices, and dramatically lowering well-being in the developing world, for food and oil were being managed for the benefit of the speculators rather than for their true purpose (feeding people and providing energy). This is an example of individual wealth being "created" without improving total output or social well-being. The rest of the economy, and especially the world's poor, were valued only to the extent that they could be used in a manner that creates profits for the financial sector. Such a globalisation is supposed to unite markets, but increasingly it has divided people.

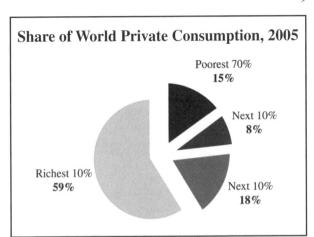

**Share of World Private Consumption, 2005**

Poorest 70%
**15%**

Next 10%
**8%**

Richest 10%
**59%**

Next 10%
**18%**

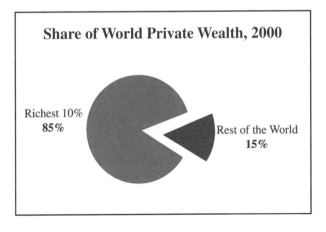

**Share of World Private Wealth, 2000**

Richest 10%
**85%**

Rest of the World
**15%**

## Effects of globalisation

While globalisation has had many successes, no one can doubt that the benefits have not been evenly or universally shared. Given that the richest 10% consume 59% of the world's goods and services, and own 85% of the world's wealth, Christians need to pause and ask themselves: are current economic relations and insitutions promoting the authentic development and participation of all God's children? Is the abundance of the few creating the scarcity faced by the many? Does such a system stand up to our understanding of justice and fairness? Does it stand up to God's justice as revealed in Holy Scripture?

However, it is not merely "the cries of the poor" that call out for God's justice. Equally troublesome is the excesses of consumerism and the "overabundance" of the affluent; the modern-day idolatry that drives markets and motivates individuals and businesses, blinding them to the suffering of the poor and to their own spiritual suffering. Consumerism is a futile attempt to fill our natural longing for the infinite, with an infinite amount of what is finite. We substitute fast cars, expensive clothing and large houses for a deep relationship with God. As physical beings we have natural needs which are satisfied by natural things: thirst (water); hunger (food); protection from the elements (shelter). All of these needs are easily satiated. What we perceive as a longing for more things, more money, more of everything, is really our longing for God displaced onto the material world. What is finite can never take the place of what is infinite, for as St Augustine has said: "Thou hast formed us for thyself, and our hearts are restless till they rest in thee." We have created "a style of life which is presumed to be better when it is directed toward 'having' rather than 'being', and which wants to have more, not in order to *be* more, but in order to spend life in enjoyment as an end in itself" (*CV*, n.36). Our "conspicuous consumption" however, creates scarcity for the poor who are unable to meet their basic needs. The empty stomachs of the poor are too often matched by the empty souls of the rich.

## A crisis of meaning

The financial meltdown and current global economic crisis have exposed the underlying instability of an economy where wealth creation for the few came at the expense of improving the well-being of the many.[14] The unbalanced financial system was merely a reflection of an unbalanced economy, which itself reflected unbalanced lives and unbalanced values. There are many factors and forces behind the rise in economic inequality and instability, yet they can all be traced back to a "crisis of meaning" (Healy & Reynolds 2009). In the pursuit of wealth we have reorganised: our economy; our work place; our family structure; our systems of education; our private values and public morals; our understanding of community and the common good; our political institutions and how we govern ourselves; who counts as a person; our definition of life; our criteria for truth; in short, who we are and what we believe in. Underlying this transformation is the belief, the faith, that individual choice is the only value; with the obvious supposition that the accumulation of material wealth, which increases the volume and variety of choices, is *the* way to promote universal happiness.

Even before the financial crisis hit the world economies, many people were questioning the emptiness of the "good life," pointing out that recent increases in wealth have not led to increases in our perceived quality of life and greater well-being. Magazines and newspapers carried articles with titles like "If the economy is up, why do I feel so down?" Technology had connected us in millions of ways, yet people felt more isolated and alone. The idea that we can create "virtual communities" with the ability to choose with whom we associate, of finding people just like us, is an extension of the ideology of choice and the religion of self (creating God in our image). By disengaging from those we actually live with, we are left with an emptiness that only real communities, real human contact, and ultimately only God, can fill. After a generation of pursuing wealth under the delusion that it would make us happier, we have created an unbalanced economy which, when it crashed, left us with neither wealth nor happiness. The worship of money, wealth and possessions has once again proven to be idolatry. "Having" is not a good substitute for "being".

This "crisis of meaning" requires a re-examination of the ancient topic of riches and poverty, of what is wealth and how it is created and distributed, and why poverty amid affluence persists. The problem (existential or otherwise) of the current crisis is not that material wealth was created, distributed and used. These are all necessary aspects of how societies solve the "economic problem" (or how they provide for their material well-being). The current crisis has its roots in how wealth was created and the disconnection between wealth and well-being, in the concentration of wealth in fewer and fewer hands and in the wasteful manner in which wealth was used. All of these problems stem from seeing wealth as the end or final purpose of all economic and social activity, instead of as *means to higher ends*.

## Wealth creation *versus* economic inequality

The question of how wealth is created, who receives the benefits of its creation (i.e. who is rich and poor) and to what ends it is used, as well as the implications of rising economic inequality on the social, political and economic stability of the economy and society, are perennial and emotionally charged. They are unpleasant issues because they are ripe with envy and guilt and raise issues of exploitation, marginalisation and injustice. Professional economists concern themselves with the issues of economic growth, inflation and unemployment. These are important issues, but as Christians we must also ask the deeper questions about who we are as individual people and communities, who counts as a person and ultimately how do our economic lives affect our relationship with God. Thus to understand these issues we need to combine the social sciences with theological reflection; the social sciences, so that we understand the reality of wealth and poverty, and theological reflection, to ground our understanding of wealth and poverty, in what promotes real and sustainable human happiness, prosperity, truth, and justice.

Prophets and philosophers have long recognised the ethical problems of such glaring inequalities. Socrates and Plato saw wealth and poverty as two sides of the same "evil coin"; the overindulgence of the rich was seen as the cause of scarcity for the poor, with both wealth and poverty encouraging anti-social behaviour and attitudes.[15] Increasingly, social scientists have come to recognise that rises in wealth and income inequality, constitute a major economic, social and political problem, contributing to international and internal conflicts, environmental degradation and economic stagnation. Pope Benedict XVI alludes to this when he says "the elimination of world hunger has also, in the global era, become a requirement for safeguarding the peace and stability of the planet" (*CV*, n.27).

To Christians, the existence of extreme inequality of wealth and income presents a special challenge, for the Gospels call us to see these issues as more than just "economic" problems. Is God's creation meant for all or just for a few? Does God's call to human solidarity place any obligations on those who own and control the "wealth of nations?" For followers of Jesus, all economic questions presuppose that union with God is our ultimate end, thus our evaluation of the creation, distribution and use of wealth is from the perspective of how wealth can promote or retard this union.

Furthermore, this perspective fully recognises that we achieve union with God through and with others. Christians necessarily reject the extreme individualism which is so prevalent today: theologically (all that matters is my relationship with God); ethically (do what fits my personal values) and economically (I am responsible for myself alone). Scripture teaches us that God's covenants (through Abraham, Noah, Moses and Jesus) are with "a people", not with specific individuals. Ethics gives us guidance and rules for living in communities, and we can only create wealth in communities by working with others, for as individuals we are all poor.

## Further insights

To address this crisis of meaning we will apply the theological, philosophical and economic insights of the

Catholic Social Thought tradition to the issue of income inequality and the many problems that rising inequality causes. By grounding our analysis in Catholic Social Thought we address directly the crisis of meaning. By placing the empty promises of materialism in juxtaposition with the eternal values of the Gospel we expose the limitations of an economy grounded in scarcity, while at the same time highlighting God's promise of abundance. Thus our analysis is grounded in the problems of the here and now, but is not limited by the belief that here and now is all there is.

We are following Pope Leo XIII's advice: "There is nothing more useful than to look at the world as it really is - and at the same time to look elsewhere for a remedy to its troubles" (*RN*, n.14). Furthermore, following Cardinal John Henry Newman, we recognise that economics requires answers to ethical questions which economics as a discipline cannot answer. Economics is helpful in thinking about how to achieve specific goals, but it cannot guide us as to which goals are moral, honourable and good, and which are not. We need to go to the higher disciplines of philosophy and, especially, theology, to guide us in choosing what goals promote "integral human development."[16]

## The Catholic Social Thought tradition

Unfortunately, the Catholic Social Thought tradition has gained the nickname "the Church's best-kept secret."

Until recently most Catholics knew very little about it (in fact, many seminaries still do not include it as part of priestly formation). While elements from Catholic Social Thought may crop up in statements from the Bishops' Conference on "faithful citizenship" or the "common good", or in the mission statements of Catholic charitable institutions, one rarely hears of these principles otherwise.

The purpose of Catholic Social Thought is to bring the values of the Gospel into our economic and social lives. As Pope John Paul II observed:

> The teaching and spreading of her social doctrine are part of the Church's evangelising mission. Since it is a doctrine aimed at guiding people's behaviour, it consequently gives rise to a 'commitment to justice,' according to each individual's role, vocation and circumstances. The condemnation of evils and injustices is also part of that ministry of evangelisation in the social field, which is an aspect of the Church's prophetic role. (*Sollicitudo Rei Socialis*, n.41).

Similarly, Pope Benedict XVI has made explicit the link between love, as charity, and social action for justice:

> Love - *caritas* - is an extraordinary force which leads people to opt for courageous and generous engagement in the field of justice and peace... This dynamic of charity received and given is what gives rise to the

Church's social teaching, which is *caritas in veritate in re sociali*: the proclamation of the truth of Christ's love in society. (*CV*, nn.1, 5).

The Church has a legitimate role in promoting social justice, not only in the hearts of Christians, but also in the structures that make up society, for structures greatly influence behaviour and outcomes.

Catholic Social Thought flows from the two great Commandments: *Love God with all your heart*, and *love your neighbour as yourself*. The Church lives these two commandments in her sacramental and liturgical life and in her promotion of social justice. Both are essential aspects of the Church's mission. They are not competing missions, but instead are two sides of the same coin. Liturgy without social justice is empty, for it is not *lived* (as St James tells us: "faith by itself, if it has no works, is dead" (*Jm*, 2:17)). Works without faith, in the long run, are also empty, for they will lack the necessary focus on authentic human flourishing grounded in real social justice. To promote authentic human flourishing requires a real and deep understanding of the dignity of each human person, of the *Imago dei*, of being created by God in His image and likeness. As the Catechism states:

2419 "Christian revelation... promotes deeper understanding of the laws of social living." The Church receives from the Gospel the full revelation of the truth about man. When she fulfils her mission of proclaiming the Gospel, she bears witness to man, in the name of Christ, to his dignity and his vocation to the communion of persons. She teaches him the demands of justice and peace in conformity with divine wisdom.

## The way of life

Catholic Social Thought is not a "third way", the long-sought-after middle ground between the extreme individualism and alienation of capitalism and the collectivism and lack of freedom of communism. It is instead based on "the Way," with the goal of informing Christians how to bring a Christian perspective to the economic and social issues they face. As one of the earliest Christian texts, *The Didache* or *The Teachings of the Twelve Apostles* (AD 50-120) states:

"The Way of Life is this: first, love the God who made you; secondly, your neighbour as yourself: do not do to another what you do not wish to be done to yourself… The Way of Death is this. First of all, it is wicked and altogether accursed: murders, adulteries, lustful desires, fornications, thefts, idolatries, magical arts, sorceries, robberies, false testimonies, hypocrisy, duplicity, fraud, pride, malice, surliness, covetousness, foul talk, jealousy, rashness, haughtiness, false pretensions… Of men that have no heart for the poor, are not concerned about the oppressed, do not know their Maker; of murderers of children, destroyers of God's image (procurers of abortion)" (pp.15-18).

## The Church's teachings

The continuity in the moral teachings of the Church since the time of the Apostles is clear to be seen here. The Church does not claim to have a unique expertise on the economy, finance, business, politics and the environment (all areas that have changed considerably in the past 2000 years). All these important areas have their unique disciplines and experts, and we cannot minimize their contributions. Yet each of these disciplines needs to be grounded in ethical principles, and this is what Catholic Social Thought offers, principles that can guide our economic and social actions and choices and criteria for evaluating outcomes. As Pope John Paul II noted: "[Catholic Social Thought is] an application of the word of God to people's lives and the life of society, as well as to the earthly realities connected to them, offering 'principles of reflection,' 'criteria of judgment,' and 'directives for action'" (*SRS*, n.8).

## Guidance for Christians

Catholic Social Thought tradition has elaborated a set of principles that are designed to guide Christians in their social and economic lives, promoting virtuous behaviour and social justice. As regards human beings, its two core principles are: 1) the protection of human dignity; and 2) the promotion of the common good. All the other principles are elaborations on these. It should be noted that these are complementary and not competing principles; they reinforce each other and are not to be seen as two competing goals to be balanced against each other. You cannot increase the common good by decreasing human dignity. Pope John Paul II noted their interconnectedness:

> "The dignity of the human person is a transcendent value, always recognised as such by those who sincerely search for the truth. Indeed, the whole of human history should be interpreted in the light of this certainty. Every person, created in the image and likeness of God (cf. *Gn* 1:26-28), is therefore radically oriented towards the Creator, and is constantly in relationship with those possessed of the same dignity. To promote the good of the individual is thus to serve the common good, which is the point where rights and duties converge and reinforce one another" (*World Day of Peace Message*, 1999).

Christian anthropology (the Christian view of human nature) asserts that each and every person is a unique individual with a social nature, so that the well-being of the individual is tied up with the well-being of the community. From these come other principles of Catholic Social Thought: the Principle of Participation; the Universal

Destination of Goods; the Preferential Option for the Poor; the Right to Work; the Right to Private Property (along with the social responsibility of private property); Subsidiarity and Solidarity. We will see that these principles inform our understanding of rich and poor.

---

### Principles of Catholic Social Thought

*(1) Dignity of the Human Person*

Each and every person is a unique individual with a social nature. The dignity of each and every person comes from their being made in the image and likeness of God (*Imago Dei*), and as this dignity is a gift from God it does not lessen due to age, disability, income status, gender or race. "There is neither Jew or Greek, there is neither slave nor free, there is neither male nor female; for you are all one in Christ Jesus" (*Ga* 3:28).

*(2) Principle of Participation*

As the development of the person is only brought about through social interaction (working with others, and giving oneself to others), participation in social processes is a fundamental human right (as it immediately flows from the nature of the human person). Participation is a good in and of itself. Furthermore, it is both a human right and a human duty (part of one's social obligations to the community).

*(3) Principle of the Common Good*

*"The principle of the common good, to which every aspect of social life must be related if it is to attain its fullest meaning, stems from the dignity, unity and equality of all people.*

---

According to its primary and broadly accepted sense, *the common good* indicates 'the sum of those conditions of social life which allows social groups and their individual members relatively thorough and ready access to their own fulfillment'

(*GS*, n.26)" (*CSD*, n.163). The common good is not the sum total of individual goods, for it encompasses the good of all people and the whole person in relationship.

### (4) The Universal Destination of Goods

"God intended the earth and all that it contains for the use of every human being and people. Thus, as all men follow justice and unite in charity, created good should abound for them on a reasonable basis" (*GS*, n.69). "God gave the earth to the whole human race for the sustenance of all its members, without excluding or favouring anyone. This is the foundation of the universal destination of the earth's goods." (*CSD*, n.171). All rights of property (including intellectual property), are subordinate to the rights of all to subsistence.

### (5) Preferential Option for the Poor

"The principle of the universal destination of goods requires that the poor, the marginalised and in all cases those whose living conditions interfere with their proper growth should be the focus of particular concern" (*CSD*, n.182). The development of the person is blocked by exclusion from participation in the economic spheres of social life (poverty). Poverty caused by exclusion extends to the social, cultural and spiritual spheres of life.

---

*(6) The Principle of Subsidiarity*

The principle of subsidiarity states that larger entities should not assume the roles and functions of smaller entities unless it is absolutely necessary. It "protects people from abuses by higher-level social authority and calls on the same authorities to help individuals and intermediate groups to fulfill their duties" (*CSD*, n.187). The unwarranted assumption of roles and functions by larger authorities often lessens social participation and should only be undertaken to increase participation.

*(7) The Principle of Solidarity*

The necessary interdependence of social life needs to be grounded in an authentic concern for the well-being of all people. This is true for those we have direct interaction with as well as for those whom our actions will affect, even if we never see them. The principle of solidarity is "a firm and persevering determination to commit oneself to the common good. That is to say to the good of all and of each individual, because we are all really responsible for all" (*SRS*, n.38).

---

In this introduction, we have briefly examined the situation regarding the rich and the poor in the 21st century. In the following part, we will look at how the Church views riches and poverty, contrasting the Gospel view with the contemporary materialist perspective. In last part of this text, we will look at some guidelines from the Christian tradition for responding to these problems, that is, creating, distributing and using wealth in a way the protects the dignity of all and promotes the common good.

# Rich and Poor: a Christian Perspective

*"For you know how generous our Lord Jesus Christ has been: he was rich, yet for your sake he became poor, so that through his poverty you might become rich"* (2 Co 8:9).

St Paul's juxtaposition of rich and poor in his second letter to the Corinthians would have been perfectly understandable to first century Christians, and to the poor of the 21st century, yet Paul reverses the usual causality. For most of human history individuals or groups that became rich did so at the expense of the poor. Typically wealth was "created" by taking a portion (small or large) of the wealth or property of "the masses" and redistributing it to a small elite. This was well understood by all. We see this in how Empires have become rich in history (taking the wealth of the conquered lands, either in the form of direct theft or taxation and tribute). The fact that the wealth of the rich often comes from the sweat and toil of the poor was even recognised by Adam Smith, the founder of modern economics: "Whenever there is great property, there is great inequality. For one very rich man, there must be at least five hundred poor, and the affluence of the few supposes the indigence of the many" (Smith 1776, p.710). St Paul's statement catches our attention because he is suggesting that many (or all) can become rich by one man becoming poor. This is contrary to human experience.

St Paul, of course, is offering a deeper understanding of the terms "rich" and "poor." Too often modern Christians read into St Paul, and the Bible as a whole, a "health and wealth" gospel, as if the inspired word of God were really a manual for economic and financial success.[17] Jesus is rich because he is God, the source of all that is. Jesus is real wealth and real well-being. Quoting Deuteronomy, Jesus tells the devil that "man shall not live by bread alone, but by every word that proceeds from the mouth of God" (*Mt* 4:4). As the Word made flesh, Jesus is the very wealth that can make everyone rich. Jesus is offering a view of riches which is the opposite of the worldly view, one grounded in abundance rather than scarcity. God's love is abundant, it has no limits. Thus from One all can be rich.

The worldly view of wealth, especially prevalent today, is that wealth is based on scarcity. A person is rich if they own things which are scarce, meaning that many more people want them than can have them, and their value is directly related to their scarcity. This is the view of wealth Adam Smith had in mind. This "economic" definition of wealth states that wealth consists of assets that yield an income or that can be exchanged for an income. Wealth and profits can grow by increasing scarcity, which is normally contrary to the common good.

Pope Benedict XVI is helpful on this point: "Profit is useful if it serves as a means towards an end that provides a sense both of how to produce it and how to make good use of it. Once profit becomes the exclusive goal, if it is produced by improper means and without the common good as its ultimate end, it risks destroying wealth and creating poverty." (*CV*, n.21).

## What is wealth?

Wealth is not a natural phenomenon; it is a social creation. It is not like gold or silver, two precious metals that are often considered as wealth, for gold and silver exist and have natural properties independent of how they are used or what we think of them. How any given society understands wealth and categorises objects as representing "wealth" is largely the result of the prevailing economic, political, social and religious attitudes of the time, in particular the "economic spirit;" "that complex inner attitude, conscious or subconscious, in virtue of which a man acts in a certain determined manner in business matters" (Fanfani, 1955, p.21).

The pre-capitalist conception of wealth was that of a "social instrument," a means to an end, with the intermediate end being sufficiency, and the ultimate end being salvation. The creation of wealth was restricted by the need to obey not only the civil law (forbidding theft, blackmail etc.) but also the moral law limiting possessions to what is needed to support one's station in life. As Amintore Fanfani has noted: "the primary characteristic of the pre-capitalist spirit is that the choice of means of acquiring goods is determined by criteria, not of pure utility, but of utility only in so far as is compatible with the vigorous existence of extra-economic criteria" (*ibid.*, p.25). The capitalist spirit does not place any such limit. It has created a new moral code which is purely economic, and which views the accumulation of wealth as the highest goal.

The pre-capitalist view of wealth, however, placed restrictions on the use of wealth.

> "This limitation might be spontaneous or enforced; it implied conformity to social morality, which was guaranteed either by the laws of the Church or by civil laws. It implied also a limitation in favour now of the supernatural ends of the individual, now of the natural ends of society, but always at the expense of natural-individual, or more exactly, of purely economic ends" (*ibid.*, p.28).

The capitalist economic spirit views any such restrictions as an infringement on natural rights, and places a single duty on the use of wealth - that it be used "rationally," that is, to maximize individual utility, either by consumption or by investment (to make even more wealth).

At the same time, it is important to separate the market from capitalism; markets and market-based economies have existed from time immemorial, and are not necessarily capitalistic. Markets, as long as they are set up properly, and the actors within them aim to act justly, are an important part of a healthy economy, as Pope Benedict XVI has noted in *Caritas in Veritate*,

> "Admittedly, the market can be a negative force, not because it is so by nature, but because a certain ideology can make it so. It must be remembered that the market does not exist in the pure state. It is shaped by the cultural configurations which define it and give it direction. Economy and finance, as instruments, can be used badly when those at the helm are motivated by purely selfish ends. Instruments that are good in themselves can thereby be transformed into harmful ones. But it is man's darkened reason that produces these consequences, not the instrument *per se*. Therefore it is not the instrument that must be called to account, but individuals, their moral conscience and their personal and social responsibility" (n.36).

## Why wealth matters

The reason wealth creation, distribution and use are significant factors in the economy is because the performance of the overall economy depends on the efficient use of the productive assets that comprise much of a nation's "wealth."

A large portion of this wealth consists of capital goods (factories, machinery and tools) that promote current and future production and financial wealth that will direct future investment. It is important that these assets be used in an efficient manner, yet this prompts the question - *what is efficiency?* A common-sense definition of efficiency would evaluate means according to their effectiveness at achieving desired ends. Thus, from the perspective of the individual stockholder, efficiency is measured in terms of rising share prices or dividends. For the firm, efficiency is often measured as the return to the shareholder (if one takes the narrow shareholder view of corporate responsibility), but there may be other goals that are more important to the wider community of 'stakeholders'. Politicians and economists often define efficiency for the country in terms of economic growth, yet there are many things that promote economic growth without promoting happiness.

All these various conceptions of efficiency, however, tend to measure progress towards an end that remains unexamined. Rising share prices are not good in themselves; nor do they necessarily reflect a healthy economy. Daily attention to the performance of the stock markets is out of proportion to their importance in the real economy. Corporate profitability and economic growth are not final goals, but are themselves means to an end.[18] Concentrating on means as if they were ends is being like a driver who says "I am lost, but at least I am making good time." Efficiency is not merely how fast we are travelling on the road; it is how fast we are getting to our desired destination. And making good time (efficiency) is only worthwhile if you have a worthy destination.

Efficiency is therefore a concept that only has meaning in terms of goals or ends; it measures our success in achieving those goals or ends. As Pope Benedict XVI as said, "One of the greatest challenges facing the economy is to achieve the most efficient use - not abuse - of natural resources, based on a realisation that the notion of "efficiency" is not value-free" (*CV*, n.50).

## Christian view of riches

There are five themes regarding wealth or riches that run right through the 2000-year-old Catholic Social Thought tradition (from the Bible to the modern papal encyclicals): (1) wealth is a gift from God; (2) riches can be a distraction from our true purpose (union with God); (3) God's creation is for all, thus riches should be widely shared; (4) moral obligations adhere to the creation and use of wealth; and (5) material riches are subservient to heavenly riches.

The first theme is that wealth is a gift from God. In Deuteronomy we are told to remember the true source of wealth: "You may say to yourself, 'My power and the strength of my hands have produced this wealth for me.'

But remember the LORD your God, for it is he who gives you the ability to produce wealth" (*Dt* 8:17-18). As Pope John Paul II stated in *Centesimus Annus*: "The original source of all that is good is the very act of God, who created both the earth and man, and who gave the earth to man so that he might have dominion over it by his work and enjoy its fruits" (*CA*, n.31).

While God is the source of all wealth, man is called to be a co-creator, and actively to work to create more wealth. The Apostle Paul stated the importance of man contributing to production in the most stark terms: "If any will not work, neither let him eat" (2 *Th* 3:10). Thus "Social justice implies that persons have an obligation to be active and productive participants in the life of society and that society has a duty to enable them to participate in this way" (*EJA*, n.71).

Pope John Paul II taught that work is essential not only for its contribution to the community's well-being, but also to the development of the worker: "Work is a good thing for man - a good thing for his humanity - because through work man not only transforms nature, adapting it to his own needs, but he also achieves fulfilment as a human being and indeed in a sense becomes 'more a human being'" (*LE*, n.9).

Our call to work flows from our being made in the image of God. Often, however, we create structural barriers that prevent people participating in the production process.

"The fact is that many people, perhaps the majority today, do not have the means which would enable them to take their place in an effective and humanly dignified way within a productive system in which work is truly central. They have no possibility of acquiring the basic knowledge which would enable them to express their creativity… thus, if not actually exploited, they are to a great extent marginalised" (*LE*, n.33).

## Wealth and love of God

The second theme is the warning against replacing the love of money for our love of God. We see this vividly described in Ezekiel (28:4-10), but the best summary of this view is from Jesus Christ: "No one can serve two masters; for either he will hate the one and love the other, or he will be devoted to the one and despise the other. You cannot serve God and mammon (riches)" (*Mt* 6:24).

The Christian virtue of detachment from worldly possessions does not imply that possessions are evil, as we will see later on, but instead is a call to place nothing between ourselves and God. Thus when Jesus (*Lk* 18:18-23) told the rich man that if he wanted to follow Him he had to sell all his possessions and give the money to the poor, He did so because He saw that the rich man's possessions were preventing him from becoming a disciple. Jesus also saw that wealth could be a barrier even, stating that it would be easier for a camel to go through the eye of a needle then for a rich man to enter the kingdom of God. Reflecting on the relationship between wealth and happiness, Pope John Paul II noted (*SRS*, n.28):

> A disconcerting conclusion about the most recent period should serve to enlighten us: side-by-side with the miseries of underdevelopment, themselves unacceptable, we find ourselves up against a form of "superdevelopment", equally inadmissible, because like the former it is contrary to what is good and to true happiness. This "superdevelopment", which consists in an excessive availability of every kind of material goods for the benefit of certain social groups, easily makes people slaves of "possession" and of immediate gratification, with no other horizon than the multiplication or continual replacement of the things already owned with others still better. This is the so-called civilisation of "consumption" or "consumerism," which involves so much "throwing-away" and "waste." An object already owned but now superseded by something better is discarded, with no thought of its possible lasting value in itself, nor of some other human being who is poorer.

Consumerism and "superdevelopment" creates scarcity for the poor as the rich eat up larger and larger shares of the world's natural resources. The growing "conspicuous consumption" of the rich is also *the* major cause of environmental problems such as global warming. While many are quick to blame "overpopulation" for the environmental crisis, a quick look at the facts shows that this is not the case. The high polluting countries are mostly the rich countries, and the fact that China has passed the United States of America as the world's biggest emitter of carbon dioxide is due more to its doubling of its *per capita* emission rate than its population growth. We should not be surprised that the countries that consume the most also pollute the most. Furthermore, much of the pollution in poor countries is to support exports to rich countries. The rain forests in Brazil are not being cut down to raise cattle to feed poor people, but instead to supply beef to the fast food industries in the rich countries.

## Wealth distribution

The third theme is that wealth needs to be widely shared. In Catholic Social Thought this is called the Principle of the Universal Destination of Goods. According to Pope Pius XII, social justice requires us to look at the relationship between wealth and the community as analogous to that of blood to the body: "Wealth is like the blood in the human body; it ought to circulate around all the members of the social body."[19] Hoarding wealth is harmful to the community and especially the poor.

Commenting on the rich man who wanted to build bigger barns to store his hoarded wealth (*Lk* 12:17-18), the great Church Father St John Chrysostom stated: "For when his harvest was abundant, he said to himself, 'What shall I do? I will pull down my barns, and build larger ones.' There is nothing more wretched than such an attitude. In truth he took down his barns; for the safe barns are not walls but the stomachs of the poor."[20]

The modern popes have followed the Church Fathers in their call for greater equality. Pope Leo XIII wrote in *Rerum Novarum* "the earth, though divided among private owners, ceases not thereby to minster to the needs of all" (*RN*, n.7). In *Quadragesimo Anno* Pope Pius XI wrote:

> "Each class, then, must receive its due share, and the distribution of created goods must be brought into conformity with the demands of the common good and social justice. For every sincere observer realises that the vast difference between the few who hold excessive wealth and the many who live in destitution constitute a grave evil in modern society" (*QA*, n.58).

Of course the popes and Church Fathers are following the lead set by the Apostle Paul (2 *Co* 8:13-15), when he told the new Christians that they should strive for equality: "I do not mean that others should be eased and you burdened, but that as a matter of equality your abundance at the present time should supply their want, so that their abundance may supply your want, that there may be equality."

## Wealth versus ethics

The fourth theme is on the need for wealth to be created in an ethical fashion; that it is wrong to enrich oneself at the expense of others, especially the poor.[21] The theologian Gustavo Gutiérrez (1988, p.167) summarises the many times this point is made in the Old Testament:

> The prophets condemn every kind of abuse, every form of keeping the poor in poverty or of creating new poor. They are not merely allusions to situations; the finger is pointed at those who are to blame. Fraudulent commerce and exploitation are condemned (*Ho* 12:8; *Am* 8:5; *Mi* 6:10-11; *Is* 3:14; *Jr* 5:27; 6:12), as well as the hoarding of lands (*Mi* 2:1-3; *Ezk* 22:29; *Hab* 2:5-6), dishonest courts (*Am* 5:7; *Jr* 22:13-17; *Mi* 3:9-11; *Is* 5:23, 10:1-2), the violence of the ruling class (2 *K* 23:30, 35; *Am* 4:1; *Mi* 3:1-2; 6:12; *Jr* 22:13-17), slavery (*Ne* 5:1-5; *Am* 2:6; 8:6), unjust taxes (*Am* 4:1; 5:11-12), and unjust functionaries (*Am* 5:7; *Jr* 5:28).

Gutiérrez goes on to note that the Bible does not simply object to the ill-treatment of the poor. "[I]t is not simply a matter of denouncing poverty. The Bible speaks of positive and concrete measures of preventing poverty from becoming established among the People of God. In Leviticus and Deuteronomy there is very detailed legislation designed to prevent the accumulation of wealth and the consequent exploitation" (*ibid.*). As the *Catechism* states: "The seventh commandment enjoins the practice of justice and charity in the administration of earthly goods and the fruits of men's labour." (*CCC* 2450-63) Pope John XXIII emphatically stated that the rules of justice apply to the creation of wealth:

> Justice is to be observed not merely in the distribution of wealth, but also in regard to the conditions under which men engaged in productive activity have an opportunity to assume responsibility and to perfect themselves by their efforts. Consequently, if the organisation and structure of economic life be such that the dignity of workers is compromised, their sense of responsibility is weakened, or their freedom of action is removed, then we judge such an economic order to be unjust, even though it produces a vast amount of goods whose distribution conforms to the norms of justice and equity. (*MM*, n.82-83)

### Spiritual treasure

The final theme is the statement that material wealth is secondary to heavenly treasures. Aristotle, using natural reason, argued that wealth has to be seen as a means to an end, and not as an end in itself.

For Christians the final end is union with God, thus wealth is good if we use it in a way that brings us closer to God and bad if it becomes a barrier to God. Our true goal and the source of real happiness is the beatific vision in heaven and not earthly riches. "Do not lay up for yourselves treasures on earth, where moth and rust consume and where thieves break in and steal, but lay up for yourselves treasures in heaven, where neither moth nor rust consumes and where thieves do not break in and steal. For where your treasure is, there will your heart be also" (*Mt* 6:19-21).

Jesus tells us that our salvation is tied to how we treat the poor and marginalised (*Mt* 25:31-46). According to the Catholic Social Thought tradition, those who have control of wealth carry a special responsibility. Pope Leo XIII warns that "those whom fortune favours are warned that freedom from sorrow and abundance of earthy riches are no guarantee of that beatitude that shall never end, but rather the contrary; that the rich should tremble at the threatening of Jesus Christ - threatening so strange in the mouth of our Lord; and that a most strict account must be given to the Supreme Judge for all that we possess" (*RN*, n.18). "[I]t is one thing to have a right to the possession of money, and another to have a right to use money as one pleases" (*RN*, n.19).

The right of private property is always restricted by our social responsibility to use it towards the common good. Part of the "right use of money" is the duty of charity, to give to those who are less fortunate out of one's surplus. Later social encyclicals have extended this duty of charity into a duty to change the unjust social structures that create inequality (which in turn creates the need for charity).[22]

## Private property

The Church has always supported the right to private property, but, like all other rights, this one implies duties. It is not an absolute right and needs to be subordinated to the higher end of the "universal destination of material goods." As Pope Paul VI stated: "All other rights whatsoever, including those of property and of free commerce, are to be subordinated to [the principle of the universal destination of goods]. They should not hinder but on the contrary favour its application. It is a grave and urgent social duty to redirect them to their primary finality" (*PP*, n.22). It is not enough, as Pope John XXIII argued, "to assert that man has from nature the right of privately possessing goods as his own, including those of productive character, unless, at the same time, a continuing effort is made to spread the use of this right through all ranks of the citizenry" (*MM*, n.113).

## Results of market fluctuations

Economists often argue that markets should be allowed to determine incomes, for incomes are prices and it is important for prices to reflect real economic variables. Yet not all markets are competitive, and actual prices are often due to something more than economic variables, for example the influence of economic and political power. Such effects on higher and lower wages, rents and profits can act as market signals that encourage the sellers of labour, land and capital to use their resources more productively (in a manner which yields them the highest rate of return).

Seeking the highest rate of return is good for the community at large, but only when it encourages entrepreneurs to produce the goods that are most wanted by consumers. Pope John Paul II, addressing the role of profits, emphasises that they too are a means to higher ends, and are not to be seen as ends in themselves:

"The Church acknowledges the legitimate role of profit as an indication that a business is functioning well. When a firm makes a profit, this means that productive factors have been properly employed and corresponding human needs have been duly satisfied. But profitability is not the only indicator of a firm's condition. It is possible for the financial account to be order, and yet for the people - who make up the firm's most valuable asset - to be humiliated and their dignity offended... Profit is a regulator of the life of a business, but it is not the only one; other human and moral factors must also be considered which, in the long term, are at least equally important for the life of a business" (*LE*, n.35)

This was also an important theme in *Caritas in Veritate*.

It is questionable that current levels of income inequality are the result of blind market forces, for markets always have to operate within a social, political, legal and cultural context. Economic and political power always influence income levels, sometimes raising those of the poor (such as with minimum wages and social welfare payments), but more often raising the incomes of the economically and politically powerful. Those whom governments have "bailed out" during this financial crisis (banks, financial speculators, insurance industry, large corporations) are the usual beneficiaries of government policy. The real issue is not whether the government should or should not influence income levels, because just about everything it does affects someone's income. The question we should ask ourselves is whether government policy promotes more or less income equality.

## Christian view of poverty: poverty is exclusion

Most definitions of poverty refer to the inability of individuals or groups to meet their basic needs. Disagreement arises over the definition of "basic need." Economists tend to define needs in exclusively materialistic and economic terms, whereas Christian anthropology recognises the social nature of the person, adding the need to participate in the economic and social life of the community as a human right. The "principle of participation" states:

> (*CCC* 1879) The human person needs to live in society. Society is not for him an extraneous addition but a requirement of his nature. Through the exchange with others, mutual service and dialogue with his brethren, man develops his potential; he thus responds to his vocation.

This recognises that a person is more than just an economic actor, and that happiness and well-being are determined by social, political, cultural and spiritual factors as well as economic ones. While basic economic needs are primary (since if these are not addressed adequately the others will not be either), this does not mean that meeting them is all that is necessary for promoting happiness and well-being. Human dignity requires more than basic economic minimums.

Poverty and the treatment of the poor are fundamental concerns for the Catholic Social Thought tradition. This concern for the poor was so important to the early Church (*Ac* 4:32-37; 6:1-6) that one of her first actions was setting up relief for the poor. We also see that part of St Paul's evangelising mission included raising money for the "saints" in Jerusalem (*Rm* 15:25-33). "The Church, from her origins and, in the contemporary era, through the Encyclical *Rerum novarum*, has proclaimed and practiced *a preferential option for the poor*, considering it a 'special form of primacy in the exercise of Christian charity'" (John Paul II, Message for the 43rd Italian Catholic Social Week, November, 1999).

For the Christian, the "option" for the poor is not optional. Working to help the poor is "proof of [the Church's] fidelity to Christ" (*LE* n.8). The centrality of this to a Christian understanding of the economy comes from the importance Jesus gave the poor in His mission and message, from the outset: "The spirit of the Lord is upon me, because he has anointed me to preach good news to the poor..." (*Lk* 4:18).

Christians help the poor not just because Jesus told us to,[23] but also because we recognise that we are all "poor" at some point in our lives and will be in need of assistance. When we are very young, when we are old, when we get sick or when we fall on hard times, we are dependant on the assistance of others. Our poverty as individuals and our interconnectedness is part of the human condition. Thus we find the "option for the poor" taught (if not lived) consistently, over our 2000-year history.

## Church's views on poverty

It may seem that the Church has a schizophrenic attitude to poverty. On the one hand we are told "blessed are the poor," yet on the other, we are told "woe" to the rich person who has caused their poverty. The Church praises the voluntary poverty of those who place God above the pursuit of material riches, who store up their treasures in heaven rather than on earth; yet she deplores the poverty that is caused by injustice and greed. But in reality there is a profound difference between these two kinds of poverty. Those who are "poor in spirit" do not allow material positions to come between them and God and their desire to do his work; while involuntary poverty is imposed on the poor, usually to the benefit of the rich, blocking their development and the promotion of their authentic happiness. It is one thing to choose freely to embrace "Lady Poverty", as St Francis called her, in order to witness to the fact that, at the end of the day, our true and everlasting "wealth" and well-being is God himself, and quite another to have material poverty imposed on whole groups in society. This is especially so where children and their development is involved; the Church has never encouraged parents to adopt voluntary poverty in the way that celibate priests or some religious orders may do. Parents need economic means to make sure their children can grow to full maturity.

The modern Catholic Social Thought principle of the option for the poor is built upon two other important principles: those of participation and solidarity.

As we have seen, CST argues that participation in the economic, social, political, cultural and religious life of the community is essential for the development of the human person. This is part of our social nature. To the extent that poverty is caused by exclusion it becomes a barrier to the authentic development and happiness of persons.

The principle of solidarity recognises the interdependence of all persons. We all naturally recognise that we are dependent on our family members, co-workers, neighbours and those with whom we interact, yet the Christian idea of solidarity broadens this to all humanity. As Jesus noted (*Lk* 6:32-36), even sinners love those who love them. Christians are called to a higher standard, to love all, as Jesus loved them.

> The exercise of solidarity within each society is valid when its members recognise one another as persons. Those who are more influential, because they have a greater share of goods and command services, should feel responsibility for the weaker and be ready to share with them all they possess. Those who are weaker, for

their part, in the same spirit of solidarity, should not adopt a purely passive attitude or one that is destructive of the social fabric, but, while claiming their legitimate rights, in their turn, should not selfishly insist on their particular interests, but respect the interests of others. (*SRS*, 39)

The poor are excluded by other individuals, by social institutions ("structures of sin") and by actions which are taken by the poor themselves, often out of ignorance or despair. If social participation is essential to the growth and development of each human person, any action which results in social exclusion is a violation of the natural law.

"It remains true, however, that every form of externally imposed poverty has at its root a lack of respect for the transcendent dignity of the human person. When man is not considered within the total context of his vocation, and when the demands of a true "human ecology" are not respected, the cruel forces of poverty are unleashed" (Pope Benedict XVI, 2009).

# Wealth and Well-Being;
# Promoting Authentic Human Development

*If the problem of happiness were solved by
economic comfort, the classes who are more
comfortable would be happy, which is absurd.*
G. K. Chesterton

Few can doubt that we have been in a period of economic
transition. The financial collapse has shown that many
aspects of the "new economy," so widely praised just a
few years ago, are unstable and unsustainable. For years
we were told that we had entered a brand new world of
unlimited financial possibilities, brought about by
sophisticated techniques and technologies, starting with
the internet and the information technology revolution,
spread through the world by "globalisation" and managed
by "financial engineers" who, armed with the tools of
financial derivatives, could eliminate risk and uncertainty.
Now we can see that the new financial structure was a
house of cards built on sand, where speculation replaced
enterprise, and the self-interest of many financial
speculators came at the expense of the common good.

While there were many factors that contributed to the financial meltdown of 2008, they start with the exclusion of ethics from economic and business decision making. The designers of the new financial order had complete faith that the "invisible hand" of market competition would ensure that the self-interested decisions of market participants would promote the common good. In practice the market did not turn private vice into public virtue. Even when markets are well designed and working efficiently, they do not always harmonise private and social costs and benefits, for not everything that contributes to human flourishing can be acquired through the marketplace. As Pope John Paul II noted, many important human needs do not have a market voice. Many of these moral considerations were not part of the discussion when financial markets were deregulated. Excluding moral factors led to imprudent decision-making and the undervaluing of systemic risk. The recent economic crisis is a moral problem not only because of its implications (bankrupt business, lost savings, unemployment, and poverty), but also because its causes can be traced to the exclusion of moral values from economic decision-making.

How to respond? There is no space here for technical details, as important as these are. Instead, we can put forward six guidelines for a response to the "crisis of meaning" that come out of the Christian tradition, and in doing this we are especially helped by the timely encyclical of Pope Benedict XVI, *Caritas in Veritate*.

## 1: Grow in love

The poor are the forgotten and excluded members of our societies, and their lives are largely invisible. Our response needs to start here, and Pope Benedict XVI gives us the key for doing so when he opens his encyclical with the dramatic and blindingly simple statement that love is an "extraordinary force" that drives us to work for "justice and peace" (*CV*, n.1). Our underlying problem, then, is a lack of love. This is not a soppy feeling, but a powerful force that, working through the virtues of courage and generosity, fills us with the energy, devotion and perseverance needed to attack these deep-rooted problems. It is a love that is illumined by truth - directing its energies towards what really constitutes genuine human development. It is the love of the richer people in society for the poor, and for their dignity; and of the poorer for the rich, and their need to find true meaning in life. It is a love that drives both rich and poor to play their parts in rectifying the current intolerable situation.

## 2: Share your faith

Love is at the core of our faith - God is love, St John tells us - and so, if the problem of growing injustice and inequality can be traced back, ultimately, to a lack of love in our society, then sharing our faith - evangelisation - helps to spread that culture of love upon which true human development can be built. Sharing one's faith is a good thing in itself, of course, and a duty of all Christians, but here it is important to underline its relevance for tackling the injustices in society. *"The Gospel is fundamental for development*, because in the Gospel, Christ, 'in the very revelation of the mystery of the Father and of his love, fully reveals humanity to itself'" (*CV*, n.18, italics original). Here Pope Benedict XVI underlies another important aspect of faith-sharing for development - the example of Christ reveals to us what is the good human life and what authentic human development means. Sharing faith here includes both offering the riches of our faith to others as something in which they can come to share as believers like us, and also, in the context of interreligious dialogue, searching together for an ever-deeper understanding of, and closeness to, the source of divine love in the world. The latter is so necessary today for promoting peace, without which development is hardly possible.

### 3: Development as our vocation

Love is the central part of our calling as Christians, and since love drives us to work for justice, so development is part of that calling too. But more than this, development is to our natural human nature what our vocation is to our spirit, to our life of faith. As Pope Benedict XVI says, picking up on Pope Paul VI:

Man does not develop through his own powers, nor can development simply be handed to him. In the course of history, it was often maintained that the creation of institutions was sufficient to guarantee the fulfilment of humanity's right to development. Unfortunately, too much confidence was placed in those institutions, as if they were able to deliver the desired objective automatically. In reality, institutions by themselves are not enough, because integral human development is primarily a vocation, and therefore it involves a free assumption of responsibility in solidarity on the part of everyone (*CV*, n.11).

The positive and effective interaction between freedom, responsibility and good institutions is crucial if we are to promote human development. If we see work for development as part of our vocation - that is, our calling to live in love with God - we are all the more likely to invest the time, hard work and effort needed to make that positive interaction happen.

There is more to say here, and not surprisingly, Pope Benedict XVI helps us say it:

The Christian vocation to this development therefore applies to both the natural plane and the supernatural plane; which is why, 'when God is eclipsed, our ability to recognise the natural order, purpose and the "good" begins to wane'... if all reality were merely history and culture, and man did not possess a nature destined to transcend itself in a supernatural life, then one could speak of growth, or evolution, but not development (*CV* nn.18, 29).

Without the transcendental or supernatural dimension, we have great difficulty in determining what is truly human development. Though our contribution as Christians will often be rebuffed, we need to offer to our brothers and sisters the deeper insights that we gain from our faith. These can help guide all people of goodwill towards a deeper and more authentic view of human development.

## 4: Work from the "value and substance of things"

The order in the natural world, including the kind of nature that we as human beings have, is a guide to how we should work for development, since development is about realising the potential that is in living beings, and most importantly, in human beings. The whole idea of "development" (as opposed to, say, "progress") presupposes that there is something to develop, that there is something that needs to unfold and realise itself. Furthermore, working from nature is the most "democratic" and "fair" thing to do, since it represents a check on any powerful group in society hijacking the development agenda for its own ends. And yet, taking nature as a guide for what constitutes authentic or true development is not yet accepted in the mainstream. Rather, development is linked to freedom from constraint whereas nature is seen as a constraint on freedom. At the same time, thanks to our growing acceptance that we must treat our environment not just as we please, but according to its nature if we are not to destroy both our environment and ourselves, the mainstream consensus may begin to change; we should not underestimate the enormous transformation in our way of thinking and acting that this implies.

The need to promote human development according to the nature of human beings ties the question of development to that of respect for human life in all its stages (see *CV* n.28). Working from the substance and value of things means adopting a consistent ethic of life, where the promotion of a culture favouring life means both protection for the child in the womb and a chance to live and develop for a child suffering hunger and want.

## 5: Avoid simplistic solutions

We have criticised here the current dominant problem in society: the substitution of means for ends, and the tendency to focus on efficiency and competition while forgetting the reason for them. At the same time, it can be a temptation for those of us within the Church, especially if we are very aware of this problem, to make the opposite error, and not to pay enough attention to the means of achieving the ends we believe in. We can jump towards what seem obvious solutions to us, but which turn out to be simplistic. It is too easy either to condemn or to exalt various technical solutions to the problems of development. There is no point in idealising or in demonising technology. All instruments can be used for good or ill. Pope Benedict XVI has interesting comments on this to make in *Caritas in Veritate*:

Technology, viewed in itself, is ambivalent. If on the one hand, some today would be inclined to entrust the entire process of development to technology, on the other hand we are witnessing an upsurge of ideologies that deny *in toto* the very value of development, viewing it as radically anti-human and merely a source of degradation. This leads to a rejection, not only of the distorted and unjust way in which progress is sometimes directed, but also of scientific discoveries themselves, which, if well used, could serve as an opportunity of growth for all. The idea of a world without development indicates a lack of trust in man and in God. It is therefore a serious mistake to undervalue human capacity to exercise control over the deviations of development or to overlook the fact that man is constitutionally oriented towards "being more". Idealising technical progress, or contemplating the utopia of a return to humanity's original natural state, are two contrasting ways of detaching progress from its moral evaluation and hence from our responsibility. (*CV*, n.14)

We need to keep in mind the value of the social and technical sciences, and to use them properly in finding solutions to the dramatic problems that face us.

### 6: Build up community

Whatever particular technical models or economic solutions we can find to the inequality and exclusion of poverty, and to the "superdevelopment" of the rich, strengthening the bonds of relationship and community around us will be important to their success. This means building up our families and our local communities, but also creating community in the worlds of business and economics; parts of our life together in society that we have seen hitherto as being competitive and individualistic. We need the development of a more "civil" society in all its senses - a society that cultivates those virtues that support community and social living. As Pope Benedict XVI says, traditional networks of solidarity need to be strengthened (he mentions especially workers' organisations), but we also need to create new forms of business and enterprise in the economic sphere for the expression of fraternal love and reciprocity.

This brings us to a point we already made: all wealth is created in communities of work, between people - nobody can create wealth entirely on their own. By ourselves we can produce very little, much less a surplus beyond our basic needs. Our standard of living has risen only through collective action, through cooperation more than through competition, working in groups to achieve much more than the sum total of our individual capabilities. Individual initiative is certainly important, yet we cannot deny the fact that our individual well-being owes more to where and when we were born, and the social networks we are part of, than to our own individual efforts and talents. We may pride ourselves that what we have is our just dessert, what we have earned, but at all times God and our fellow humans are co-creators with us. These reflections also lead us back to one of the key points of this text: the importance of the distribution of wealth, and the need to do so in a way that supports networks of fraternity and solidarity.

# A Concluding Comment: Unbalanced Economy / Unbalanced Lives

*"What does the Lord require of you but to do justice, and to love kindness and to walk humbly with your God"* (Mi 6:8)

Most economic and social problems, past and present, individual and collective, have their origin in a lack of balance. The existence of the rich and the poor are the visible manifestation of this lack of balance. The collapse of banks and other financial institutions has been due to a lack of balance between seeking reward and avoiding risk. Extreme fluctuations in currencies (the rise or fall in value of the pound, euro and dollar) have been due to a lack of balance in international trade and investment. The decline in share prices and the volatility of stock markets are the result of an imbalance between money invested and actual productive activities carried out by the money raised for investment purposes. And economic stagnation and decline in the real economy, with its corresponding increases in unemployment and decreases in standards of living, has been caused by an imbalance between the "financial sector" and the real economy. Too much of the nation's "time, talent and treasure" has been spent gambling on the financial markets for short term gain, and too little was spent improving the real purpose of business, making goods and services that promote economic well-being.

## Imbalance in our lives

Corresponding to the lack of balance in the "macro-economy" has been the equally significant lack of balance in our individual lives. The pursuit of wealth and income often came at the expense of family and friends. A higher level of consumption was paid for by spending less time with family. This is particularly harmful for our children, who were given a seemingly endless supply of gadgets as a substitute for parental time and attention. The affluent society (Galbraith, 1959), with its endless possibilities, became instead the over worked and over-stressed society (Schor, 1993). We had become rich in goods and poor in everything else.

The cause of the imbalance in our lives is the diminished role we allow for God. Instead of being at the centre of all we do, He is often only given an hour or so on Sunday, and increasingly excluded altogether (rise of atheism), or trivialised in new age spirituality. How many times have we heard someone say "I am not religious, I am spiritual." When you ask them what being spiritual means, you often get answers that sound like a dialogue from Star Wars. Spirituality has come to mean recognition of a higher power, yet that higher power can be whatever we want it to be, not what God has revealed to us.

Without God as the focal point our lives spin out of control, chasing every crazy whim or fashionable trend. Without God as our compass we can only see the here and now. Should we be surprised that household debt has risen so dramatically?

60

Having lost a sense of the eternal future (the afterlife), we are less able to plan and prepare for the more immediate future. In fact, any delay to our gratification (material goods, sex) ceases to make sense. Intermediate goods become final goods. We use up the resources the future will need and leave future generations to clean up our mess, or worse yet, we kill the future generations, our own flesh and blood, when they are inconvenient. Jesus is the fulcrum upon which we need to balance everything in our lives. The steady teachings of the Church help is to keep on the right path. As G.K. Chesterton stated: "The Catholic Church is the only thing that saves a man from the degrading slavery of being a child of his age."[24]

## Culture of life over culture of death

The current problems of rising rates of unemployment and bankruptcies, foreclosures and lost wealth, out of control government deficits and shrinking consumer confidence are mere symptoms of bigger problems. The real issue is a *values* deficit. While governments debate stimulus packages, bank bailouts and re-regulation, what is most needed is a change of values, a conversion of hearts to redirect our efforts and our aspirations.

Markets reflect our values and we should not be surprised that they break down when solid values and universal truth are replaced by individualised ethics and moral relativism. "The truth" will set us free, but only if it is The Truth and not our own personal preferences dressed up as truth. Just as a central purpose of sex is to create life, the main purpose of economic activity is to promote human flourishing. Yet to suggest that either activity needs to be tied to its proper function is to challenge every aspect of our post-modern society. Twenty centuries after the birth of Jesus, Christians are still called to choose the way of life over the way of death, or as Pope John Paul II stated it, the culture of life over the culture of death.

We are certainly not the first Christians to live in pagan societies that are hostile to the values and message of the Gospel. Here, as always, it is good to look to tradition and seek guidance from those who passed the faith on to us. Thus we will end with some sage advice from the 4th Century Church Father, St John Chrysostom, who noted that living a Christian life is bound to be counter-cultural:

> When we live according to the moral principles of our faith, those around us may respond in three possible ways. First, they may be so impressed by the example of our goodness, and so envious of the joy which it brings, that they want to join us and become like us. That is the response which we most earnestly desire. Second, they may be indifferent to us, because they are so bound up with their own selfish cares and concerns; although their eyes may perceive our way of life, their hearts are blind, so we are unable to stir them. Third, they may react against us, feeling threatened by our example and even angry with us; thus they will cling even more firmly to their material possessions and

selfish ambitions, and slander us at every opportunity. Naturally, we dread this third type of reaction, because we want to live in peace with our neighbours, regardless of their personal beliefs and values. But if no one reacts to us in this way, we must wonder whether we are truly fulfilling the commandments of Christ. (1996, p.12)

---

**Other References:**

Alford OP, Helen and Michael Naughton, 2001: *Managing as if Faith Mattered* (South Bend In., University of Notre Dame Press).

Alford OP, Helen, Charles M. A. Clark, Steve Cortright and Michael Naughton (eds), 2006: *Rediscovering Abundance: Interdisciplinary Essays on Wealth, Income and their Distribution in Catholic Social Tradition* (South Bend, Ind., University of Notre Dame Press).

Anonymous, 1948 [50-80]: *The Didache or The Teachings of the Twelve Apostles,* translated by James A. Kleist, SL, (New York, The Newman Press).

Aquinas, Thomas, 1947: *Summa Theologica* (Benziger Bros. edition).

Avila, Charles, 1983: *Ownership: Early Christian Teaching* (Maryknoll, NY, Orbis).

Capgemini and Merrill Lynch, 1997-2008: *World Wealth Report,* various years.

Chrysostom, St John, 1984: *On Wealth and Poverty*; 1996: *On Living Simply.* (Liguori, Missouri: Liguori/Triumph); 1998: *On Almsgiving.*

Clark, Charles M. A., 2009, *A Christian Perspective on the Financial Crisis - American Economist,* Spring, Vol. 15, No. 1, p. 16-27; 2008a.

*What can Economists learn from Catholic Social Thought - Storia del Pensiero Economico,* Vol. 1, No. 1, pp. 25-51; 2008b.

*Economic Life in Catholic Social Thought and Economic Theory - in Catholic Social Thought: American Reflections on the Compendium,* edited by D. Paul Sullins and Anthony J. Blasi, Lexington Books, p. 77-99; 2006a.

*The Nature of Wealth (with Helen Alford, Steve Cortright and Mike Naughton) in Rediscovering Abundance: Interdisciplinary Essays on Wealth, Income and their Distribution in Catholic Social Tradition,* edited by Helen Alford, Charles M. A. Clark, Steve Cortright, and Mike Naughton. (South Bend, Ind., University of Notre Dame Press), 2006, pp.1-22; 2006b.

*Wealth as Abundance and Scarcity: Perspectives from Catholic Social Thought and Economic Theory in Rediscovering Abundance: Interdisciplinary Essays on*

*Wealth, Income and their Distribution in the Catholic Social Tradition*, edited by Helen Alford, Charles M. A. Clark, Steven Cortright, and Mike Naughton (South Bend, Ind., University of Notre Dame Press), pp.28-56; 2006c.

*Wealth and Poverty: The Preferential Option for the Poor in an Age of Affluence in Rediscovering Abundance: Interdisciplinary Essays on Wealth, Income and their Distribution in the Catholic Social Tradition*, edited by Helen Alford, Charles M. A. Clark, Steven Cortright, and Mike Naughton (South Bend, Ind., University of Notre Dame Press), pp.161-188.

Galbraith, John Kenneth, 1958, *The Affluent Society* (Boston, Houghton Mifflin).

Gutiérrez, G., 1988, *The Theology of Liberation.*

International Labor Organization (ILO), 2008, *World of Work Report 2008 - Income Inequalities in the Age of Financial Globalization*, Geneva.

Kammer, F. (1991), *Doing Faith Justice: An Introduction to Catholic Social Thought*, Paulist Press, Mahwah NJ.

Keynes, John Maynard, 1936, *The General Theory of Employment Interest and Money*, London, Macmillan.

Naughton, Michael, 1992, *The Good Stewards* (New York, University Press of America).

Newman, John Henry Cardinal, 1990, *The Idea of a University* (South Bend, Ind., University of Notre Dame Press).

Ryan, John A., 1913, *Alleged Socialism of the Church Fathers*, St Louis, B. Herder.

Schor, Juliet B., 1993, *The Overworked American: The Unexpected Decline of Leisure* (New York, Basic Books).

Smith, Adam, 1976a [1776], *An Inquiry into the Nature and Causes of the Wealth of Nations*, Oxford, Oxford University Press; 1976b [1759]. *The Theory of Moral Sentiments*, Oxford, Oxford University Press.

Stark, Werner, 1962, *The Fundamental Forms of Social Thought*. New York, Fordham University Press.

U.S. Catholic Bishops, (1986), *Economic Justice for All*, Washington, D.C.

Wray, L. Randall, 2008, *Financial Markets' Meltdown*, Levy Institute Public Policy Brief No. 94.

---

## Endnotes

[1] http://www.globalissues.org/article/715/today-over-25000-children-died-around-the-world

[2] Coniaris, Anthony M. Editor. 1988, *Daily Readings from the Writings of St John Chrysostom.* (Minneapolis: Light and Life Publishing Company)

[3] *2007 Human Development Report*, United Nations Development Program, 27th November, 2007, p.25.

[4] *Global Purchasing Power Parities and Real Expenditures.* The World Bank. 2005 International Comparison Program. August 2008.

[5] *FAO news release*, 19th June 2009.

[6] *2006 Human Development Report*, United Nations Development Program, 2006.

[7] http://news.bbc.co.uk/2/hi/business/4619189.stm

[8] *2007 Human Development Report*, United Nations Development Program, 27th November, 2007, p.25.

[9] See the following: *World Bank Key Development Data & Statistics*, World Bank, accessed 3rd March, 2008.
   Luisa Kroll and Allison Fass, *The World's Richest People*, Forbes, 3rd March, 2007.

[10] *FAO news release*, 19th June 2009.

[11] *2006 Human Development Report*, United Nations Development Program, 2006.

[12] http://www.globalissues.org/article/75/world-military-spending

[13] *Growing Unequal? Income Distribution and Poverty in OECD Countries*, (Paris: Organization for Economic Co-operation and Development) 2008.

[14] See Clark 2009, for a Christian view of the financial crisis.

[15] See Clark 2006a.

[16] Newman, John Henry. 1990.

[17] If you search the internet for books on Christianity and wealth you find dozen of these so-called Christian investment guides, with titles like *The Millionaire from Nazareth: His Prosperity Secrets for You!* By Catherine Ponder, which is actually part of a series *Millionaires of the Bible,* and very few books on the deeper meaning of wealth afforded by a Christian perspective.

[18] Alford, Helen and Michael Naughton. 2001.

[19] See Michael Naughton, *The Good Stewards* (1992), p.21.

[20] Chrysostom, 1984, p.43.

[21] "He who oppresses the poor to increase his own wealth, or gives to the rich, will only come to want" (*Pr* 22:16).

[22] Paul VI, *Populorum Progressio*, 66-75, and the U.S. Catholic Bishops, Economic Justice for All, 357-358.

[23] Although that is a good enough reason. Had he told us to make tents the Catholic Church would be the world's largest tent maker. But since he told us to care for the poor, the Church instead is the largest relief agency.

[24] Chesterton, G.K. *Why I am a Catholic.*